LEARNING HEBREW: FRUIT & VEGETABLES

Activity Book for Beginners

Learning Hebrew: Fruit & Vegetables Activity Book for Beginners

Bible Pathway Adventures® is a trademark of BPA Publishing Ltd.

ISBN: 978-1-98-858541-3

Authors: Pip Reid

Creative Director: Curtis Reid

For free Bible resources including coloring pages, worksheets, puzzles and more, visit our website at:

www.biblepathwayadventures.com

 # Introduction for Parents

Have fun teaching your children the Hebrew names for fruit and vegetables with our *Learning Hebrew Activity Book: Fruit & Vegetables*. From apple to apricot to pumpkin to pepper, there are 26 Hebrew words to teach them. Plus, plenty of opportunities for them to practice coloring and writing what they've learned. Flashcards, tracing activities, and coloring pages all make learning Hebrew fun!

This book is designed to build on the foundation laid in our activity book: Learning Hebrew: The Alphabet. We created both books to help you teach your children the basics of the Hebrew language in a fun and creative way. Children exposed to Hebrew, especially those growing in their knowledge of Torah, will gain increased Biblical understanding and a deeper love for Yah's Word.

Bible Pathway Adventures helps educators and parents teach children a Biblical Faith in a fun creative way. We do this via our illustrated storybooks, teacher packs, and printable activities – available for download on our website www.biblepathwayadventures.com

The search for Truth is more fun than Tradition!

Table of Contents

This book belongs to:

Ari

Draw something

The Hebrew Alphabet

	Modern	Paleo	Pictograph
Aleph	א	𐤀	𓃾
Bet	בּ	𐤁	☐
Gimmel	ג	𐤂	☐
Dalet	ד	𐤃	☐
Hey	ה	𐤄	𓀀
Vav	ו	𐤅	Y
Zayin	ז	𐤆	⊟
Het	ח	𐤇	☐☐☐
Tet	ט	⊗	⊗
Yod	י	𐤉	𓂭
Kaph	כ	𐤊	𐤊
Lamed	ל	𐤋	𐤋
Mem	מ	𐤌	∿∿
Nun	נ	𐤍	ς
Samech	ס	𐤎	𐤎
Ayin	ע	𐤏	◉
Peh	פ	𐤐	⬭
Tsadi	צ	𐤑	∿
Qoph	ק	𐤒	⊕
Resh	ר	𐤓	𓃀
Shin	שׁ	𐤔	ш
Tav	ת	✕	†

© BPA Publishing Ltd 2020

 # Did you know?

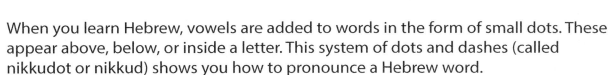

Hebrew is written and read from right to left.

Hebrew is one of the original languages of the Bible.

There are twenty-two letters in the Hebrew alphabet.

The Hebrew alphabet has no vowels.

When you learn Hebrew, vowels are added to words in the form of small dots. These appear above, below, or inside a letter. This system of dots and dashes (called nikkudot or nikkud) shows you how to pronounce a Hebrew word.

היפופוטם

✦ Agas ✦

The Hebrew word for pear is agas.
Pears grow on trees and are shaped like a tear drop.
They can be made into jams, jelly, and juice.

agas

אַגָּס

pear

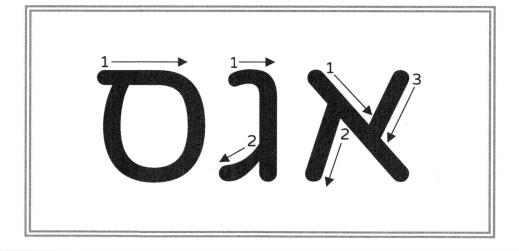

Let's write!

Practice writing this Hebrew word on the lines below.

Try this on your own.
Remember that Hebrew is read from RIGHT to LEFT.

✦ Tappuach ✦

The Hebrew word for apple is tappuach. The Israelites did not have apple orchards like we do today; instead they picked apples in the wild when they were in season.

tappuach

תַּפּוּחַ

apple

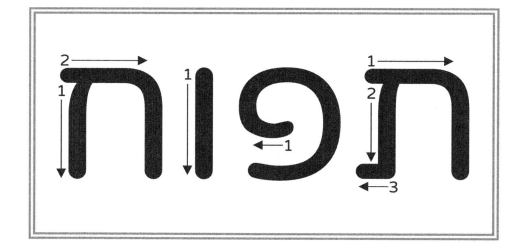

Let's write!

Practice writing this Hebrew word on the lines below.

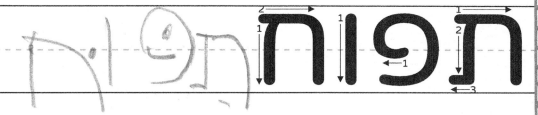

Try this on your own.
Remember that Hebrew is read from RIGHT to LEFT.

✬ Ananas ✬

The Hebrew word for pineapple is ananas.
Pineapples grow out of the ground from a leafy plant.
Did you know a pineapple can take two years to grow?

ananas

אֲנָנָס

pineapple

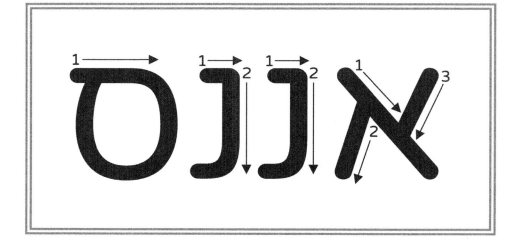

Let's write!

Practice writing this Hebrew word on the lines below.

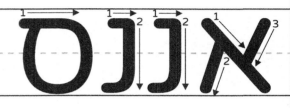

אננס

Try this on your own.
Remember that Hebrew is read from RIGHT to LEFT.

✴ Bananah ✴

The Hebrew word for banana is bananah. A banana has yellow skin on the outside and white flesh on the inside. Bananas can be used to make smoothies, clothes, and paper.

bananah

בָּנָנָה

banana

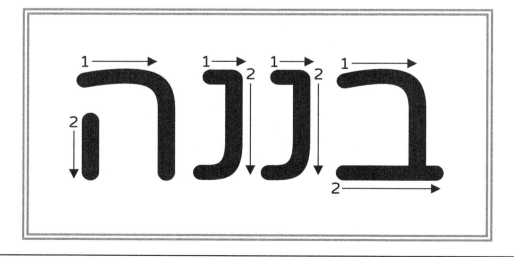

Let's write!

Practice writing this Hebrew word on the lines below.

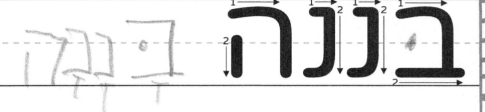

Try this on your own.
Remember that Hebrew is read from RIGHT to LEFT.

✳ Limon ✳

The Hebrew word for lemon is limon. Lemons are often used in cooking and drinks. At Sukkot, Israelites use lemons or citron to make a bouquet of leaves and fruit.

limon

לִימוֹן

lemon

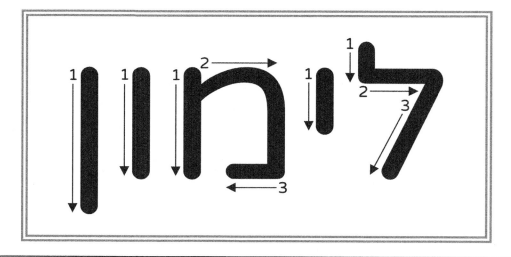

Let's write!

Practice writing this Hebrew word on the lines below.

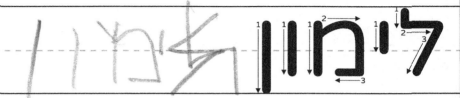

לימון

לימון

Try this on your own.
Remember that Hebrew is read from RIGHT to LEFT.

✴ Mishmesh ✴

The Hebrew word for apricot is mishmesh. The Israelites dried apricots and put them on a string or pressed them into cakes. Apricots were often eaten on long journeys.

mishmesh

מִשְׁמֵשׁ

apricot

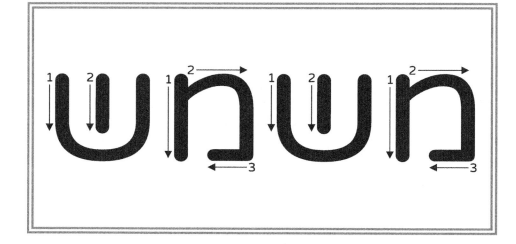

Let's write!

Practice writing this Hebrew word on the lines below.

חמש

חמש

Try this on your own.
Remember that Hebrew is read from RIGHT to LEFT.

✶ Shezif ✶

The Hebrew word for plum is shezif. Plums come in different colors and can be purple, yellow, red, green, and white. When a plum is dried, it is called a prune.

shezif

שְׁזִיף

plum

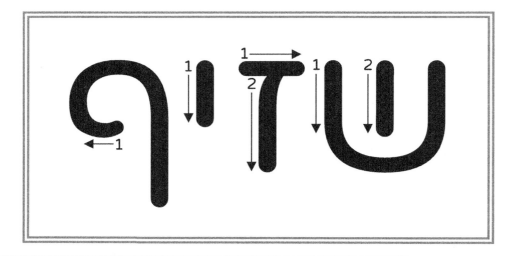

Let's write!

Practice writing this Hebrew word on the lines below.

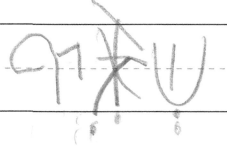 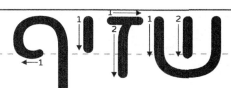

שׁדיף

Try this on your own.
Remember that Hebrew is read from RIGHT to LEFT.

✦ Tamar ✦

The Hebrew word for date is tamar. The Israelites liked to eat fresh and dried dates. They mostly used dates to make a syrup called 'date honey', which made food sweet.

tamar

תָּמָר

date

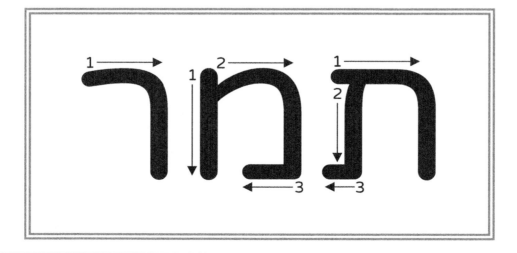

Let's write!

Practice writing this Hebrew word on the lines below.

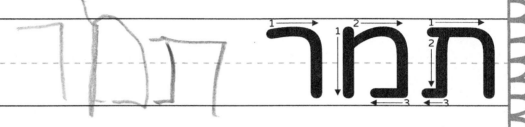

Try this on your own.
Remember that Hebrew is read from RIGHT to LEFT.

✶ Tappuz ✶

The Hebrew word for orange is tappuz. Oranges are round, have a shiny orange skin, and grow on trees. People often drink orange juice for breakfast.

tappuz

תַּפּוּז

orange

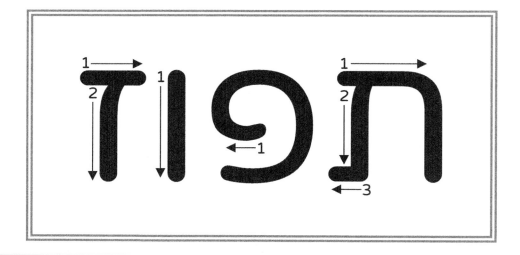

Let's write!

Practice writing this Hebrew word on the lines below.

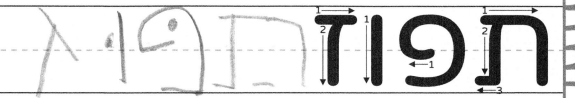

פסוד

Try this on your own.
Remember that Hebrew is read from RIGHT to LEFT.

✳ Avatiach ✳

The Hebrew word for watermelon is avatiach.
Hebrew tithing records show the Israelites often tithed
watermelons, along with figs, grapes, and pomegranates.

avatiach

אֲבַטִיחַ

watermelon

Let's write!

Practice writing this Hebrew word on the lines below.

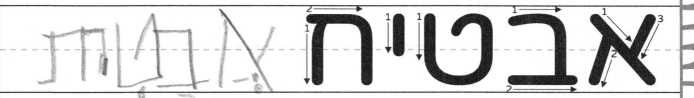

אבטיח

Try this on your own.
Remember that Hebrew is read from RIGHT to LEFT.

✶ Rimon ✶

The Hebrew word for pomegranate is rimon. Pomegranates are red on the outside and full of seeds inside. The hem of the High Priests' robe had pomegranates made from yarn.

rimon

רִמּוֹן

pomegranate

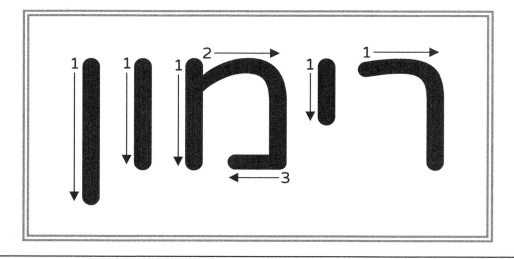

Let's write!

Practice writing this Hebrew word on the lines below.

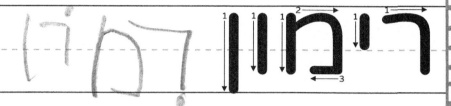

רימון

רימון

Try this on your own.
Remember that Hebrew is read from RIGHT to LEFT.

✶ Te'enah ✶

The Hebrew word for fig is Te'enah.
The Israelites ate fresh or dried figs every day.
Blocks of dried figs were sliced and eaten like bread.

te'enah

תְּאֵנָה

fig

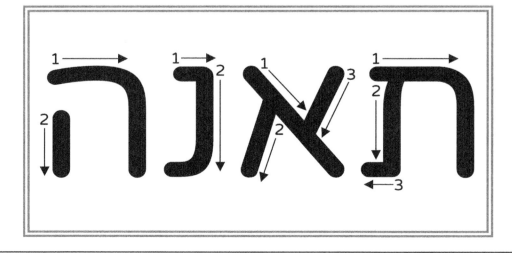

Let's write!

Practice writing this Hebrew word on the lines below.

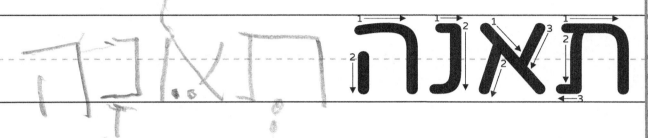

תאנה

Try this on your own.
Remember that Hebrew is read from RIGHT to LEFT.

✹ Anavim ✹

The Hebrew word for grapes is anavim. The Israelites mostly grew grapes for wine. They often took dried grapes (raisins) on long journeys or marches.

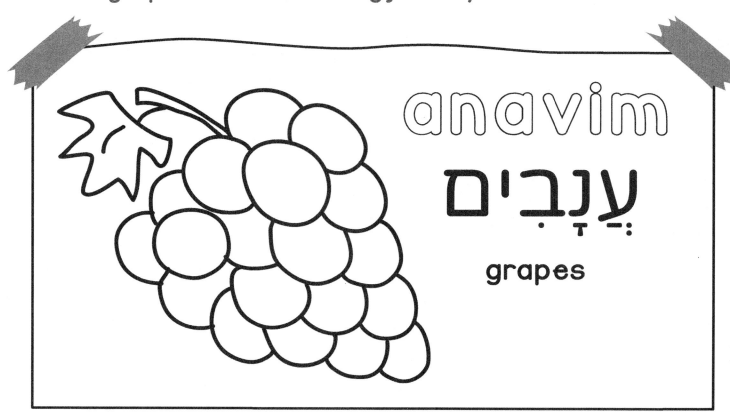

anavim

עֲנָבִים

grapes

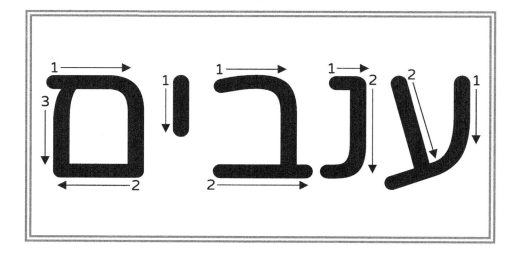

Let's write!

Practice writing this Hebrew word on the lines below.

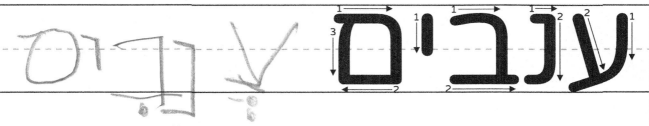

עִנָבִים

Try this on your own.
Remember that Hebrew is read from RIGHT to LEFT.

✷ Zeitim ✷

The Hebrew word for olives is zeitim. The Israelites used olive oil for food, cooking, lighting, offerings, and anointing priests and kings. Olive oil was very useful!

zeitim

זֵיתִים

olives

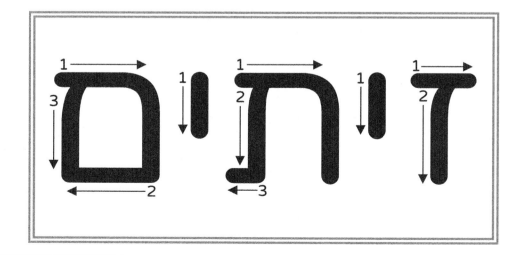

Let's write!

Practice writing this Hebrew word on the lines below.

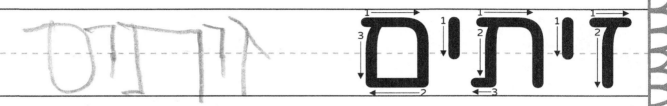

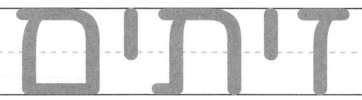

Try this on your own.
Remember that Hebrew is read from RIGHT to LEFT.

✨ Batzal ✨

The Hebrew word for onion is batzal.
The Israelites used onions to make meat and lentil stews.
They also ate uncooked onions with bread.

batzal

בָּצָל

onion

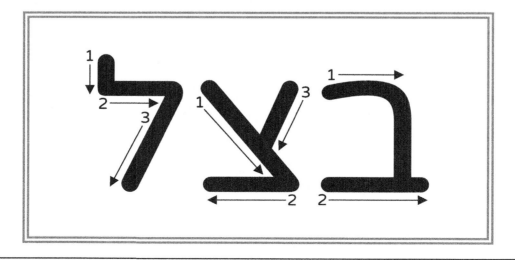

Let's write!

Practice writing this Hebrew word on the lines below.

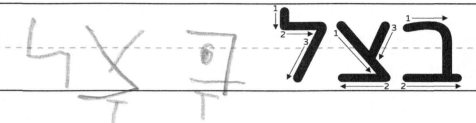

בצל

בצל

Try this on your own.
Remember that Hebrew is read from RIGHT to LEFT.

✸ Gezer ✸

The Hebrew word for carrot is gezer. Carrots are grown in the ground and are usually orange in color. The Israelites added carrots to stews and soups.

gezer

גֶּזֶר

carrot

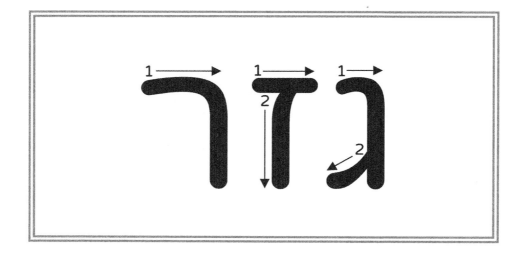

Let's write!

Practice writing this Hebrew word on the lines below.

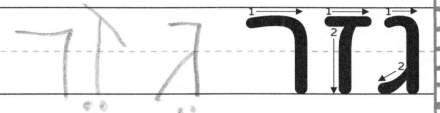

Try this on your own.
Remember that Hebrew is read from RIGHT to LEFT.

✶ Dela'at ✶

The Hebrew word for pumpkin is dela'at.
People make pumpkin into pies, salads, and medicine.
Pumpkins are grown all over the word, except for Antarctica.

dela'at

דְּלַעַת

pumpkin

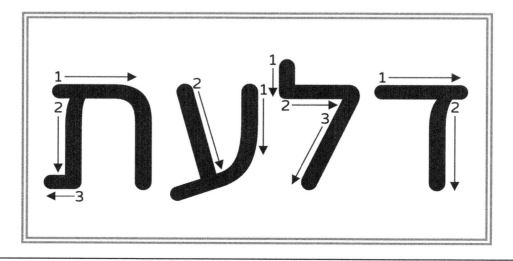

Let's write!

Practice writing this Hebrew word on the lines below.

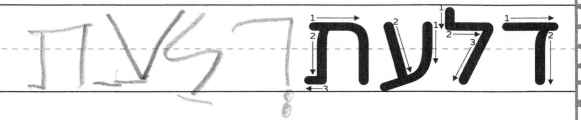

דעת‎ דלעת

דלעת

Try this on your own.
Remember that Hebrew is read from RIGHT to LEFT.

✦ Chasah ✦

The Hebrew word for lettuce is chasah.
The ancient Israelites ate wild lettuce that was bitter
and had prickly leaves. Every year, bitter herbs
are eaten at the Passover meal.

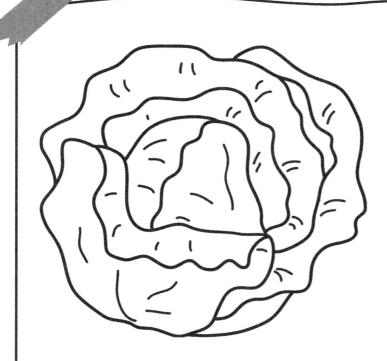

chasah

חֲסָה

lettuce

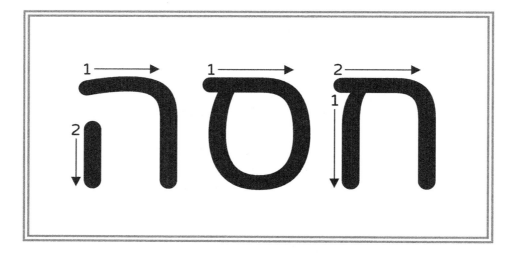

Let's write!

Practice writing this Hebrew word on the lines below.

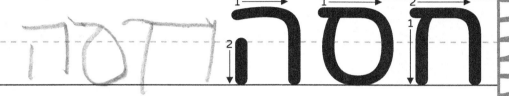

Try this on your own.
Remember that Hebrew is read from RIGHT to LEFT.

✦ Chatzil ✦

An eggplant is purple on the outside and white inside.
It is often shaped like an egg.
Eggplants are eaten in dishes all over the world.

Chatzil

חֲצִיל

eggplant

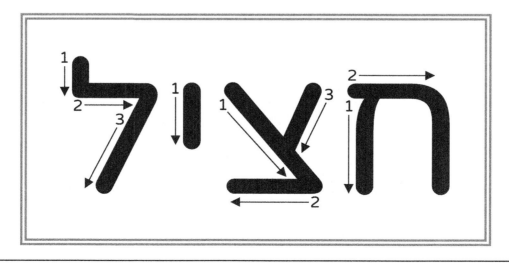

Let's write!

Practice writing this Hebrew word on the lines below.

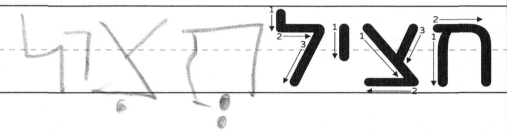

חָצִיל

Try this on your own.
Remember that Hebrew is read from RIGHT to LEFT.

✷ Keruv ✷

The Hebrew word for cabbage is keruv. Cabbage heads can be green, purple, or white. During Sukkot, some Israelites like to eat cabbage stuffed with meat.

keruv

כְּרוּב

cabbage

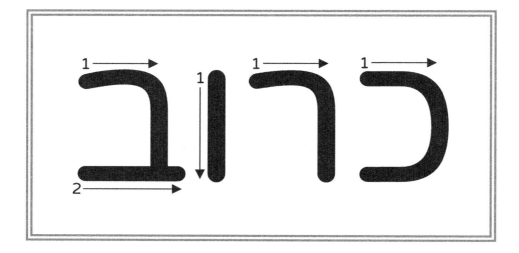

Let's write!

Practice writing this Hebrew word on the lines below.

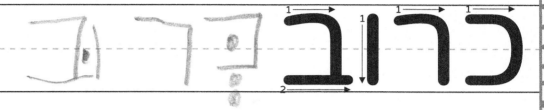

Try this on your own.
Remember that Hebrew is read from RIGHT to LEFT.

✦ Seleri ✦

The Hebrew word for celery is seleri. Celery is used to make soups and stews. Celery seeds can be used to make perfume and even medicine!

seleri

סֶלֶרִי

celery

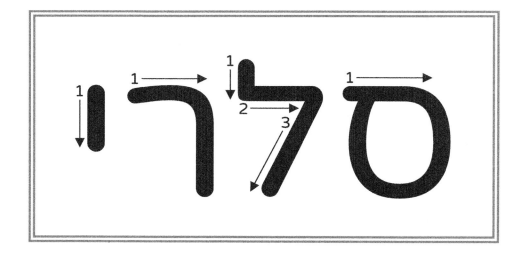

Let's write!

Practice writing this Hebrew word on the lines below.

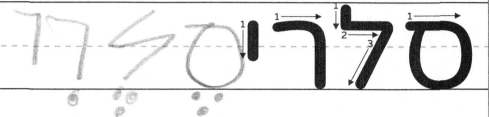

סלרי

Try this on your own.
Remember that Hebrew is read from RIGHT to LEFT.

✦ Selek ✦

The Hebrew word for beet is selek. Beets are a deep purple vegetable that grows in the ground. Some Israelites like to eat beets as part of their Passover meal.

selek

סֶלֶק

beet

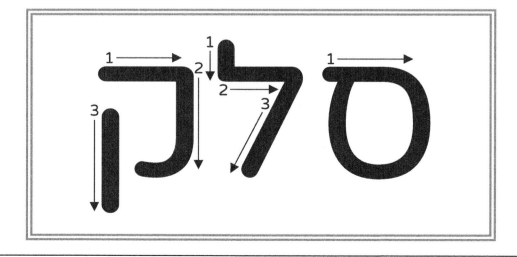

Let's write!

Practice writing this Hebrew word on the lines below.

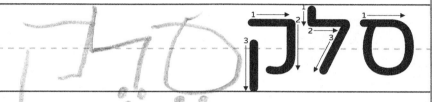

סֵלֶק

סלק

Try this on your own.
Remember that Hebrew is read from RIGHT to LEFT.

✶ Pilpel ✶

The Hebrew word for pepper is pilpel. Peppers come in many colors, including green, red, orange, and yellow. They can be eaten raw or cooked, and are good for medicine.

pilpel

פִּלְפֵּל

pepper

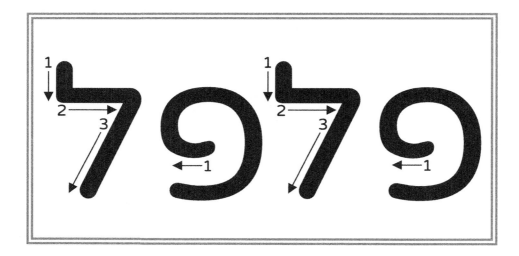

Let's write!

Practice writing this Hebrew word on the lines below.

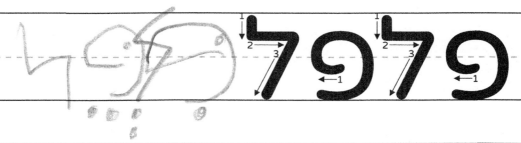

פלפל

Try this on your own.
Remember that Hebrew is read from RIGHT to LEFT.

✷ Shum ✷

The Hebrew word for garlic is shum. The Israelites used garlic and onions to add flavor to cooked food like stews. Sometimes they even used garlic for medicine!

shum

שׁוּם

garlic

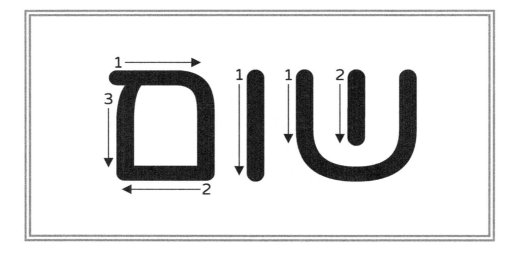

Let's write!

Practice writing this Hebrew word on the lines below.

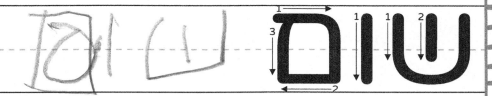

Try this on your own.
Remember that Hebrew is read from RIGHT to LEFT.

✶ Tiras ✶

The Hebrew word for corn is tiras. Corn is called maize in most countries. Did you know the yellow kernels on a piece of corn are used to make popcorn?

tiras

תִּירָס

corn

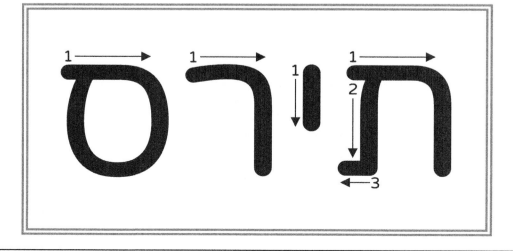

Let's write!

Practice writing this Hebrew word on the lines below.

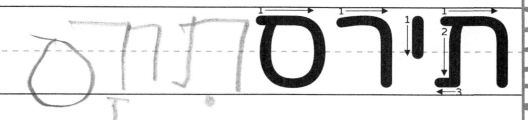

תִּירָס

תִּירָס

Try this on your own.
Remember that Hebrew is read from RIGHT to LEFT.

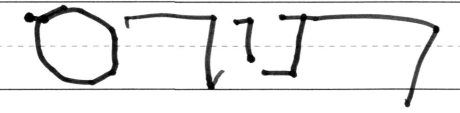

www.biblepathwayadventures.com
Learning Hebrew: Fruit & Vegetables Activity Book

✸ Tered ✸

The Hebrew word for spinach is tered. Spinach is a green, leafy vegetable. It was first grown in Persia, which is where Daniel, Mordecai and Esther lived.

tered

תֶּרֶד

spinach

Let's write!

Practice writing this Hebrew word on the lines below.

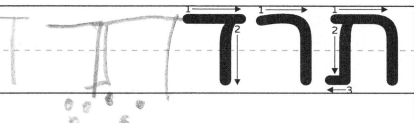

Try this on your own.
Remember that Hebrew is read from RIGHT to LEFT.

✿ Trace the Words ✿

Trace the words. Color the pictures.

⚘ Trace the Words ⚘

Trace the words. Color the pictures.

🌿 Trace the Words 🌿

Trace the words. Color the pictures.

🌿 Trace the Words 🌿

Trace the words. Color the pictures.

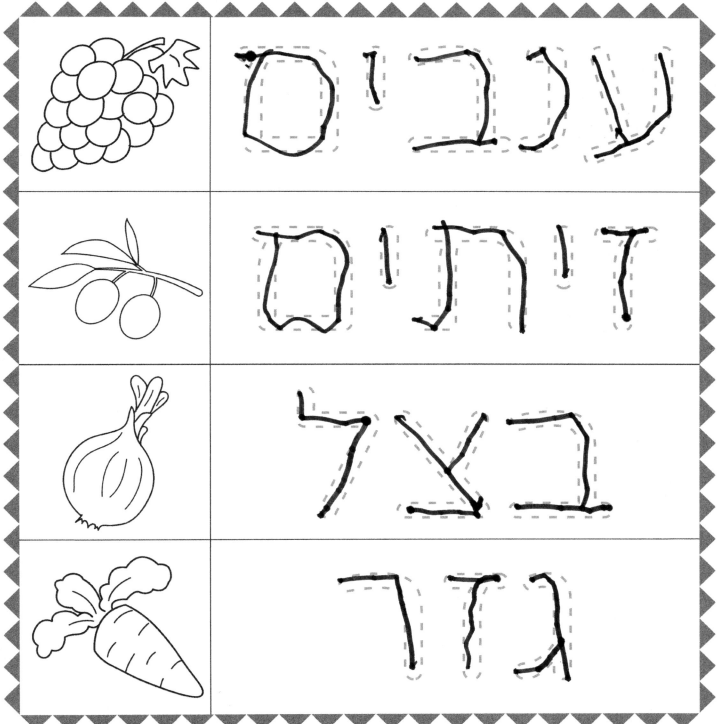

🌿 Trace the Words 🌿

Trace the words. Color the pictures.

דלעת

חסה

חציל

כרוב

🌿 Trace the Words 🌿

Trace the words. Color the pictures.

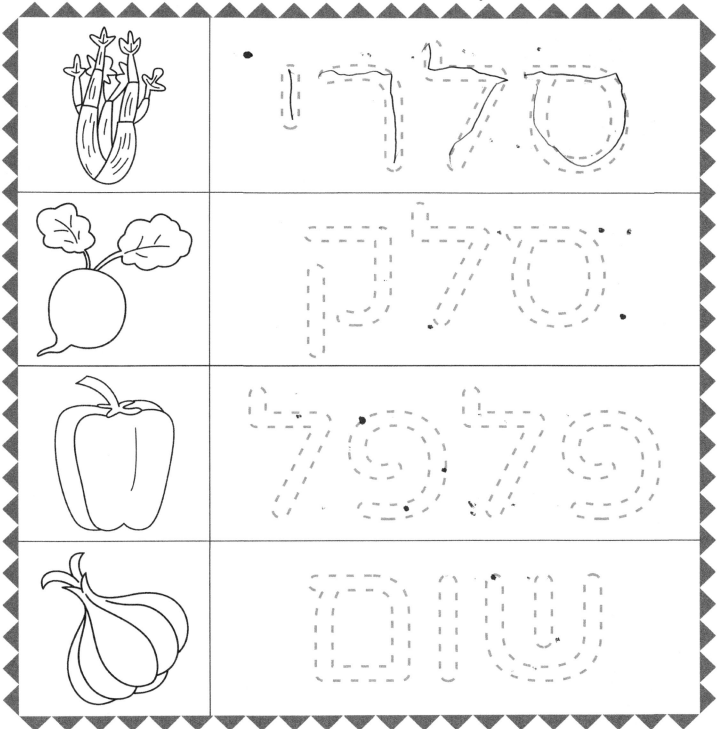

❧ Trace the Words ❧

Trace the words. Color the pictures.

FLASHCARDS

🌿 Flashcards 🌿

Color and cut out the flashcards.
Hang them around your home or classroom!

אגס

Agas / Pear

1

תפוח

Tappuach / Apple

2

אננס

Ananas / Pineapple

3

בננה

Bananah / Banana

4

לימון

Limon / Lemon

5

משמש

Mishmesh / Apricot

6

שזיף

Shezif / Plum

7

תמר

Tamar / Date

8

תפוז

Tappuz / Orange

9

אבטיח

Avatiach / Watermelon

10

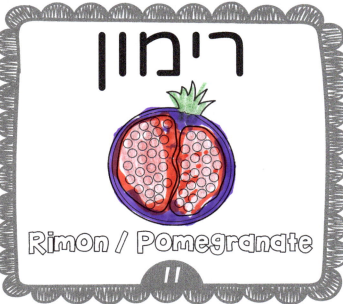

רימון

Rimon / Pomegranate

11

תאנה

Te'enah / Fig

12

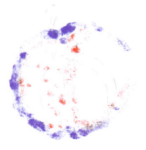

ענבים

Anavim / Grapes
13

זיתים

Zeitim / Olives
14

בצל

Batzal / Onion
15

גזר

Gezer / Carrot
16

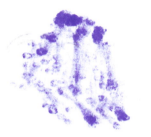

דלעת

Dela'at / Pumpkin

17

חסה

Chasah / Lettuce

18

חציל

Chatzil / Eggplant

19

כרוב

Keruv / Cabbage

20

סלרי

Seleri / Celery

21

סלק

Selek / Beet

22

פלפל

Pilpel / Pepper

23

שום

Shum / Garlic

24

תירס

Tiras / Corn

25

תרד

Tered / Spinach

26

Discover more Activity Books!

Available for purchase at www.biblepathwayadventures.com

INSTANT DOWNLOAD!

Learning Hebrew: The Alphabet
Learning Hebrew: Animals
Learning Hebrew: Around the home
Learning Hebrew: Let's Eat!
Learning Hebrew: Things that go!
Learning Hebrew: Fruit & Vegetables
Learning Hebrew: Clothes
Clean & Unclean

Printed in Great Britain
by Amazon